AMERICA AT THE CROSSROADS

KENNIKAT PRESS SCHOLARLY REPRINTS

Dr. Ralph Adams Brown, Senior Editor

Series in
**AMERICAN HISTORY AND CULTURE
IN THE TWENTIETH CENTURY**
Under the General Editorial Supervision of
Dr. Donald R. McCoy
Professor of History, University of Kansas

AMERICA
AT THE CROSSROADS

ALFRED M. LANDON'S

PROGRAM FOR AMERICAN GOV-
ERNMENT. HIS INTERPRETATION
OF THE POLITICAL, ECONOMIC
AND SOCIAL PRINCIPLES OF THE
REPUBLICAN PARTY

With an Introduction by

SENATOR ARTHUR CAPPER

KENNIKAT PRESS
Port Washington, N. Y./London

AMERICA AT THE CROSSROADS

First published in 1936
Reissued in 1971 by Kennikat Press
Library of Congress Catalog Card No: 77-137972
ISBN 0-8046-1495-4

Manufactured by Taylor Publishing Company   Dallas, Texas

KENNIKAT SERIES ON AMERICAN HISTORY AND
CULTURE IN THE TWENTIETH CENTURY

Contents

In one year since he stepped into the national spot-light Alfred M. Landon has laid a broad groundwork of fundamentals. In his public utterances gradually have taken shape a philosophy, and the major objectives of a program. Scattered through the records of the past year, rapidly accelerated in the last few months, is a story, the story of a point of view.

Here for the first time, acting with Governor Landon's approval, an attempt has been made to concentrate this point of view on the major issues now confronting the American people. As editor I have included only Governor Landon's specific statements as they were given in his own words. I have assembled and coordinated his observations and ideas on each subject without regard to when or where they were originally given. The main threads of the story remain the same, entirely unaffected by time or place.

RICHARD B. FOWLER,
KANSAS CITY, MO.

Introduction

IT IS with a sense of unusual responsibility that I take up the task of writing an introduction to the utterances of Governor Alfred M. Landon as they are concentrated on the issues now before the American people.

I believe that history will judge these utterances as one of the most important documents of the times. I say this after weighing carefully the essentials that raise any words, written or spoken, above the commonplace.

In this age or any age an important document is one that strikes into fundamentals and hits them at dead center. The powerful ideas of the times are the ideas that cut through the confusion to the basic truths. The greater the confusion the greater the premium on clear thinking. Pointless repetition of the ancient truths may be a simple recitation of platitudes, an empty echo. But to tear the essential truths out of the confusion and turn them white hot on the problems of the day is to be a powerful influence on the times.

This is what Governor Landon has done—pointedly,

inescapably, and in a language the people can understand. He has got us down to rock bottom. He is a
student of history and realizes profoundly what the
race has learned by hard knocks in the last several
thousand years. He knows that no one man, or group
of men, is smart enough to remake the world in one
generation. He knows there is nothing new in the present national undergrowth of spurious ideas. They bob
up with every generation until some clear thinker cuts
them down.

Governor Landon has made a clear and penetrating
analysis of the dangers now closing in on our hard-
earned freedom for individual enterprise. His thinking
has made clear to any man the far-reaching and devas-
tating effects of an irresponsible national administration on money matters. He has identified the forces
that, under the guise of idealism, would take away the
right of the people to rule themselves. He has set out
the major principles that must guide the nation on its
way to recovery. He has laid the groundwork for sane
and permanent standards by which we must give the
necessary protection to people in distress. He blazes a
path for steady progress instead of hysterical experimenting.

In this year 1936 we face issues as real and deep as
those that confronted the American colonists in 1776.
Governor Landon expresses himself on those issues,
not as the leader of a political party, but as an American whose roots go far down into the principles on
which this nation was founded.

A great many people in every presidential campaign
feel that both major parties offer about the same pro-

gram, differing only on a few details. That has often been the case. But this year the cleavage is deeper and more important than in the campaign of 1896. Governor Landon not only recognizes the issues, he knows how to make others see them.

Behind everything Governor Landon says is the sound experience of the race and nation. More specifically his words and ideas are backed by his own practical experience in business and government. They have been tested by him in the same troubled times that nationally produced the wave of alluring but discredited theories.

In my own experience as former governor of Kansas and a United States senator I realize how difficult it is to predict the specific problems and conditions that will confront the country in the next four years. I am not so much concerned with what a man says on these details that ordinarily pass for political issues. I am very much concerned with how the man stands on the fundamentals. If he is soundly grounded, if he knows the truth from fantasy, if he is committed to achieving the possible instead of the impossible, then I will trust him to meet the specific details at the right time.

His own utterances concentrated on the fundamental issues show very definitely where Governor Landon stands. Taken with his own record in government they should indicate the point-of-view and the manner with which he may be expected to approach the individual problems of government.

ARTHUR CAPPER,
TOPEKA, KANSAS,
SEPTEMBER 4, 1936.

AMERICA AT THE CROSSROADS

The New Frontier

THE choice ahead of the American people is not whether to keep on with the mistakes of the so-called New Deal or return to the mistakes of the old order. The old order belongs to the past but sound American principles persist. The hands of the clock of political destiny move forward, not backward. But they must turn at a steady, orderly pace. We have had too much palaver about old deals and new. Performance, to me, counts for more than phrases.

We meet the urgings of some who would solve our difficulties by changing everything; of others whose veneration for the past causes them to be shocked at the thought of changing anything.

We are aware that we must make our just contributions to the solution of the problems of the times. Each generation in turn has its own problems to solve for posterity. No age has escaped this inspiring responsibility. If such there were, then that was an age of stagnation.

In this depression as in every depression, there are

timid souls who fear that the temporary setback is to
be permanent. There is nothing to justify any such con-
clusion. We have had hard times before. They have
followed wars, or a period when our people have lost
their grip on reality and indulged in reckless specula-
tion. The day of reckoning always comes and then as
now, unfortunately, the innocent suffer with the guilty.

We are told now, however, that we got out of
previous depressions because of the natural growth of
the country and the westward expansion of the frontier.
We are warned that we are at the end of that era of
expansion and must face a new situation.

The remedy offered is that the federal government
shall restrict production, dole out jobs, and parcel out
business opportunities. This argument, instead of being
progressive, is forty years behind the times.

Much the same thing was said during the depression
of the 1890's. There was more reason for that defeat-
ist attitude then than there is now. The expansion of
our geographical frontier was slowing down. The good
farm land that could be had for the asking was about
gone. The railroads had generally been built into the
new farming areas. For a time men seemed at a loss
what to do.

We were told then, as we are being told now, that
we were at the end of an era. There was some truth in
the assertion then. There is no truth in it now. A
revival of confidence came with the election of 1896,
things began to move again. From 1896 to 1914 was
the most prosperous period that we had ever enjoyed
up to that time. Industries expanded so rapidly that

they employed not only our own workers, but millions
of workers from other countries.

A new frontier had been discovered—the frontier
of invention and new wants. Under our American way
of life, men with courage and imagination were free to
occupy this new frontier and develop it. They built a
greater America.

Our people were able to buy the new luxuries, comforts and conveniences, because they had new purchasing power—new purchasing power that came not in
checks from the Treasury, but from the production of
goods.

All this was achieved without undermining any
American institutions. It was achieved by continuing to
encourage free enterprise.

The task of the Republican party has been multi-
plied and our path to orderly economic progress
unnecessarily barricaded by social and economic experiments introduced in the last three years by the national
administration. It may be assumed that many of these
objectives were laudable, but the methods taken to
reach the objectives have tended to discredit their high
intentions. We must begin all over again.

First, to solve our problems we must understand
them. We must realize that they emerge in part from
the confused world beyond our borders. But we must
also face the fact that in a large measure these
problems arose from our own internal complexities.
Some of them come from the developments of the last
three years. Many of them were created by our swift
entry into an industrial age. We, of all the world, have
traveled farther forward in that age because we are

machine-minded, but by our very genius we have made our own troubles more perplexing. A simple order has been changed into a complex one. Nevertheless, here again we must face realities.

In Kansas we have tried to distinguish between progress and change, to evaluate change not only in its immediate effects, but in its lasting results. It is the obligation of leadership to say "yes" to some proposals and "no" to others in a manner that will not throw the country into jitters. In the solving of old problems we must avoid the creation of new ones. We must not confuse the immediate glance with the long-time view. Some roads lead to far different ends than they seemed to at the start. An innovation may be a backward step. This has been demonstrated in foreign countries where civil liberties have been yielded in return for economic security, without gaining economic security. Such a step in this country would be disastrous to all American ideas and traditions.

Yesterday, we were smug in our prosperity. Today, we are awake to the needs of an unsettled world. The West and all of America was built on faith, courage, and the homely common-sense virtues of thrift, toil and neighborly cooperation. America is willing to brave the new, to meet the changing conditions and vicissitudes of our uncertain future with determination and confidence. I bespeak for the citizens of these United States a lofty spirit of patriotism, a renewed devotion to our nation, and a new birth of individual responsibility which shall make the safety, welfare and progress of the state and nation matters of each citizen's own personal concern.

After all, experience is still the greatest teacher. From thousands of prairie firesides is handed down this homely warning: "Change does not necessarily mean progress. A social philosophy is not always bad because it is old, nor good because it is merely new."

In the progress of human rights, the road has not been continuously upward. It has not followed a straight course in the best direction. Rather, there has been a general rise with ups and downs depending upon the composite wisdom of the people. There have been curves and detours along the way where some have wandered off after false gods.

As did the pioneers, we must always keep alive the inner fire of individual conscience. We must subordinate material rewards and enthrone the things of the spirit. We need emphasis on common honesty, character, and devotion to principle.

Fumbling with Recovery

THE time has come to stop this fumbling with recovery. American initiative is not a commodity to be delivered in pound packages through a governmental bureau. It is a vital force in the life of our nation and it must be freed.

We are at the crossroads where we must make a choice between the pig-in-the-poke policies of the present administration and those American institutions under which we have enjoyed more liberty and attained a higher standard of living than any other people in the world.

To be specific, let's take the administration's record in dealing with the depression. Some people say we reached the bottom of this depression in the summer of 1932. The present administration says we reached the bottom of this depression in the spring of 1933, when it came into power. Now, if, according to the administration's own statement, it came into power at the bottom of the depression, there is only one direction we could move from that point, and that direction would be upward.

The administration at that time asked for and was given unlimited power to carry out its plans. It had the whole country pulling for it. For example, in the state of Kansas, as governor, I cooperated with it in every way possible. I felt that the nation's interest came ahead of any partisan interest. I believe that this was typical of the general attitude. In short, this administration, in the beginning, had less opposition than any administration that ever has been in power in the memory of living man. And now, in all fairness, I believe it is time for us to check results.

The present administration has made the worst record ever made in the history of the United States in bringing this country out of a depression. Never before, once we reached the bottom, did it take us so long to get out of a depression, and our recovery still is unfinished business. After more than three years with unequaled peacetime grants of power and spending, millions of our people still are unemployed, one person out of every six is on relief, and the deficit is bigger than ever. Why?

If you will look into the facts of the situation you will find that on four different occasions since March, 1933, this country has started on a definite movement toward recovery, and on each of these four occasions it was set back again by some new reckless experiment or disturbing move by the present administration. How can we feel any confidence that this won't keep on happening?

What this heedless retarding of recovery means to

people out of work, to young people coming of age, is simply tragic. What the young people of America really need, and earnestly desire, is not relief—but opportunity.

I believe that the real issue before the American people today is not whether we are better off now than we were in 1933; the real question and issue is this: Have we made as much progress in coming out of this depression as we have a reasonable right to expect?

We are going to be many years unscrambling the eggs cooked up by the kitchen cabinet of this administration. One of the greatest failings of these cooks was that they were unable to tell the bad eggs from the good. The result has been indigestion for all of us.

The country is ripe for recovery. We are far behind in expenditures for upkeep and improvements and for expansion. The total of this demand—in industry, in new enterprises, in our homes and on our farms— amounts to billions of dollars. Once all this consumer demand is released, the problem will be not where to find work for the workers, but where to find workers for the work.

One of the signs of the ending of past depressions was the launching of new business ventures. It is true that most of them were small. Altogether, however, they provided work for many millions of people. In the present depression this demand for work has not yet appeared. Few new ventures have been started. Why? Because the small businessman, the workingman who would like to become his own boss—the average American—has hesitated to start out for himself. He lacks confidence in the soundness of federal policy; he is afraid of what may come next.

We must dispel his fear, restore his confidence, and place our reliance once more in the initiative, intelligence and courage of these makers of jobs and opportunities. That is why I say, in all earnestness, that the time has come to unshackle initiative and free the spirit of American enterprise.

We must be freed from incessant governmental intimidation and hostility. We must be freed from excessive expenditures and crippling taxation. We must be freed from the effects of an arbitrary and uncertain monetary policy. And, through a vigorous enforcement of the antitrust laws, we must be freed from private monopolistic control.

Once these things are done, the energies of the American economic system will remedy the ravages of depression and restore full activity and full employment.

An illustration of the present administration's methods is in the so-called surplus tax bill jammed through Congress this spring.

This is the most cockeyed piece of tax legislation ever imposed on a modern country and if I am elected I shall recommend the immediate repeal of this vicious method of taxation.

One practical effect of this tax law is to prevent a corporation from using its earnings in the business. It must pay them out in dividends. In consequence, earnings no longer provide funds for making needed improvements, for replacing out-of-date equipment, and for additions to the plant.

Now what does this mean to a man looking for a job? It means less chance for finding work. There will not be those jobs that come from the gradual growth of our small businesses, from the replacement of equipment, and from plant expansion.

For those workers who already have jobs the effect of the tax law is just as bad.

Because of this legislation it is no longer possible for a business, except at unbearable cost, to build up a reserve for meeting future losses. In other words, a business organization, unless it already has reserves, is put on a hand-to-mouth basis.

This means that it can exist only so long as it can make a profit. Once trade slackens to the point where the business cannot make a profit, it is lost. Not having a reserve to fall back upon, its lot is bankruptcy, and the lot of the workers is unemployment.

There is one other point in this connection that I would like to mention: During the depression, private industry paid out over 20 billion dollars more than it took in—20 billion dollars that helped to cushion the depression and keep employees working. This expenditure was possible only because of reserves created during prosperous years.

Yet by careless, ill-advised tax legislation this present administration is, in effect, forbidding a restoration of the reserves exhausted by the depression.

The sponsors of this tax law may have thought it was a smart way to appear to "soak the rich." Actually it has no relation to "soaking the rich." What it does is protect the big fellow who still has a reserve, and tie a millstone around the neck of the little fellow. This legislation prevents the small businessman from expanding by the usual method of plowing earnings back into his organization. It is making harder and harder the reemployment of many of those at present out of work. And it is jeopardizing the job of every man and woman who today is working for a business corporation.

Let me add, the revision of this bill is only one of the changes needed in our tax system. Our whole tax structure, federal and state, needs overhauling.

The administration has presented no permanent solution of our major problems. On the contrary, it has created many new problems and its gross overcentralization of power reflects either ignorance or indifference in regard to our federal system of government.

We must condemn half-baked legislation, maladministration, and the dangerous short cuts to permanent change attempted in the name of emergency.

The action of the Supreme Court in cutting away some of the errors in recent national legislation has given a healthful impetus to our entire economic life. The months following the voiding of the NRA registered America's most marked upturn since the depression. In contrast, the four months following the passage of that act were marked by a drop in industrial production and employment equaled only by our greatest panics of the past.

━━

C H A P T E R   T H R E E

Changing the Constitution—Human Rights and State Rights

I TURN now to the basic principles upon which our nation is founded. America has always stood, and now stands, first of all for human rights, for "the life, liberty, and pursuit of happiness" of the great Declaration. The prime needs of men have not changed since that declaration, though new means from time to time may be necessary to meet those needs. But the great safeguards against tyranny and oppression must not be cast away and lost. They must be saved that men may live free to pursue their happiness, safe from any kind of exploitation.

Our forefathers had a passion for self-government as a corollary to the individual right of self-determination. Through this yearning for orderly national existence, security and individual liberty has come the written covenant we term the Constitution of the United States. It is the militant manifestation of great spiritual force.

It is not my belief that the Constitution is above change. The people have the right, by the means they have prescribed, to change their form of government to fit their wishes. If they could not do this, they would not be free. But change must come by and through the people and not by usurpation. Changes should come openly, after full and free discussion, and after full opportunity for the people to express their will.

Our government was founded to give life to certain vital principles. The people embodied these basic principles of human rights in the federal and state constitutions. Thus, the people themselves, of their own free will, set up this government. And it is still the government of the people. Any change which the people want they can have by following the procedure they themselves laid down.

But for any official or branch of government to attempt such a change, without authority from the people, is to do an unwarranted and illegal act. It is a substitution of personal for constitutional government. If added power is needed, the people have set out how that authority may be had from them—if they wish to give it.

This, in its broad essentials, is the basic structure of our government.

A government is free in proportion to the rights it guarantees to the minority. The Constitution was not framed to give us anything, but to protect inherent rights we already possessed. It was framed to protect minorities controlled by impulsive majorities. For a century and a half, the Constitution has protected American citizens against such oppression. Against repeated onslaught it has preserved the right of trial by jury; it has been the safeguard of the American home and of churches in their most sacred right of religious freedom; it has protected the freedom of the press; it has safeguarded individuals in their right of free speech, and it has been the guarantee of the right to conduct lawful personal affairs without interference by meddling bureaucracy. This, fellow citizens, is the Constitution which was established to make the United States a sanctuary for every honest individual and every honest interest.

Let me make this emphatic, the Constitution of the United States is not an obstacle to progress. It is the balance wheel of progress.

No flouting of the Constitution, whether by executive evasion, loose legislation or insidious propaganda, can destroy our safeguards so long as courage and common sense are cherished in the hearts of the American people.

These ancient rights remain safe today only as the Constitution stays written in our hearts. But today there are powerful forces trying to convince our people that the Constitution is not their charter of human liberties.

As our economic life has become more complex and specialized some need, real or apparent, has often been urged as an excuse for a further grant of power from the people. They have sometimes given, sometimes withheld, the desired power.

There has now appeared in high places, however, a new and dangerous impulse. This is the impulse to take away and lodge in the chief executive, without the people's consent, the powers which they have kept in their state governments or which they have reserved in themselves.

In its ultimate effect upon the welfare of the whole people, this, then, is the most important question now before us: Shall we continue to delegate more and more power to the chief executive or do we desire to preserve the American form of government? Shall we continue to recognize that certain rights reside within the people, that certain powers are reserved for the states, and that certain functions are delegated to the federal government?

Government power must always be used unflinchingly to correct the abuses and inequalities which admittedly exist. So far as possible, this should be done by the individual states or by compacts among the states. In the case of abuses beyond the power of jurisdiction of the states, federal authority should be used.

I am, however, against the transfer to Washington of any power which can be more safely and efficiently administered by state and local governments.

It is a fundamental law of representative government that nothing shall be done by a larger unit that a small unit can do as well.

It is a fundamental principle of our American system that the federal government in Washington shall have only such powers as are specifically granted to it.

The founders of our government knew all too well the evils of being governed from a distance. They knew from experience that the local colonial governments understood the needs of the colonies better than any distant government. All they asked at first was more self-government. When they found that they could not get it, they demanded independence.

That distrust of centralized power was the beginning of our American liberty. We are now asked to barter it away for persuasive theories which have been tried and found wanting.

Now I know that many of us, at one time or another, have become dissatisfied and impatient with the efforts of our local and state administrations to solve our difficulties.

At such times it has seemed to us that only a larger, more powerful unit of government could meet the need.

For those who have followed such a line of reasoning I have the understanding that comes from experience. As a young man I was attracted to the idea of centralizing in the federal government full power to correct the abuses growing out of a more complex social order. When the people rejected this alternative, I was as disappointed as anyone. But in spite of this rejection, I have lived to see many of those abuses substantially corrected by the forty-eight state legislatures in their fields and by the federal government in its field of interstate commerce.

More recently, as a small independent oil producer, I saw my industry ask for federal regulation because of a selfish exploitation of a natural resource, which, once wasted, cannot be replaced. When federal regulation failed, the industry made progress in the solution of the problem by turning to state action, supplemented with interstate compacts as provided by the amazing foresight of the makers of the Constitution.

Should destructive forces succeed in persuading the people to give up this safeguard, the American government would then become a source of oppression such as now afflicts various other peoples throughout the world.

C H A P T E R   F O U R

The American Way of Life Is Challenged

SOME people now say that the America we have built no longer meets our needs. The American way of life is being challenged. We are told that it does not meet modern requirements. They point to the unemployed. They cite examples of special privileges. They say that these are inescapable by-products of our system of free enterprise and of our form of government. They recognize, as all of us do, the lack of balance in our economic structure.

These are defects, it is true, and call for remedies. But I believe that there is more promise for their solution by clinging to American ideals than under any other plan which has been proposed.

Periods of depression are favorable for reviving ancient and discredited systems of society and of government and presenting them as the sure way of gaining Utopia. In the waste of extravagance of the boom days and the hardships of the depression, many of us went woolgathering.

So it is not surprising that the confidence of many

30

of our people in our way of doing things has been shaken. They are wondering whether we may not have to scrap our American institutions. This doubt and distrust is fostered by unstable men to whom it is always dangerous to give political power.

The basic issues of the approaching national referendum hold a deeper interest for our country than any that have arisen for a generation past. The crucial period in which we now find ourselves is testing representative government.

This feeling of doubt and distrust, like the depression, is world-wide, and not confined to the United States. It challenges not only the economic system of free enterprise, but even the representative form of government. Before the depression, such phrases as "the onward sweep of democracy" were commonplace. Now in many parts of the world democracy is in retreat and dictatorships are advancing.

Today we can well review the way of life that has brought us thus far on the road to national greatness, and ask ourselves whether the end of that road has been reached.

Let us look first at some of the attributes of our country and of our people. These are more fundamental than political issues. For out of them spring those habits of thought and of action and those social, economic and governmental institutions which create political issues.

Wherever I have gone in this country, I have found Americans. That is no idle phrase. The word "American" has come to mean something more than a dweller within our boundaries. It means an attitude of heart and mind, an outlook on life. It means not only deep love of liberty and justice, but courage to face the dangers and responsibilities that go with liberty.

Our fathers cherished this way of life because they bought it with their own blood. We have received it as a free gift from them. There is danger that we may not prize it as we should.

This freedom from the coercive hand of government has always been a distinctive feature of American life. Even before the recent revival of dictatorships, the citizens of foreign countries were subject to restrictions unknown in America. Their goings and comings were closely watched and regulated. They could not open new businesses without the consent of a bureaucratic government. Their established businesses were subject to incessant bureaucratic meddling. Economic and social development was bound to be slow under these conditions.

In contrast, the American way of life has left men and women free from these restrictions. Our people have been free to develop their own lives as they saw fit and to cooperate with one another on a voluntary basis. They have been encouraged to start any honest enterprise that would enable them to support their families, give the public the goods and services it wanted, and make jobs for themselves and others. Under this encouragement, business has expanded here faster than elsewhere, the public has had more goods; workers have had higher wages and shorter hours; children have had better school facilities; all have had higher standards of living. There has been more leisure for spiritual and cultural things.

This freedom of enterprise which has distinguished the American way of life exists not for the few, but for all. It has benefited every American whether he worked for himself or someone else. Under freedom, more enterprises are started than under government control of production. Let us not forget, however, that a fair distribution of economic and social benefits is yet to be brought about.

Now I take it that we Americans lived under a system of freedom because we wanted to live that way. We still like it better than any other way. We know there are many wrongs to right. Only the misguided will claim that this system is perfect or that all its results are desirable. We do not contend that individual effort can of itself overcome many of the handicaps placed on great numbers of individuals by the workings of our industrial civilization. The record proves, however, that our system gives the most personal liberty to human beings and offers on the whole the highest possible standard of life to the greatest numbers. It is a system which permits the driving force of free initiative to produce more of the good things of life and thus promote a more rapid improvement of human welfare than can be found anywhere outside of America.

We have found by experience that American institutions serve our purpose better than those of any other country. We not only want to safeguard our freedom, but we also want security and abundance of the good things of life. We are told, however, by defeatists that we cannot have both. We must, they say, choose between freedom and security. They insist we must give up one in order to gain the other. Let us not surrender to any such counsel of despair. Let us not abandon our determination to win security and abundance without sacrificing any of our precious heritage of freedom.

I believe the greatest need of the American people today is a revival of confidence, confidence in themselves and in their ability to work out their own problems. We find in almost every depression that there is a certain percentage of people who lose confidence in themselves. They begin to doubt whether they are really capable of getting out of the difficulties. And it is usually at this point that someone comes along with the idea of finding a superman and turning it all over to him.

We cannot go back to the days before this depression. We must go forward, facing our new problems, solving them under the old eternal verities, cherishing the American tradition of free men, surrendering the unessential for new and necessary benefits.

But just as the basis of our national life is in the soil, so is the main source of our recovery in the character of our people.

The pioneers of Kansas came to the plains seeking new homes, just as all America was built by pioneers. They were a rugged, hard-working, thrifty, courageous people. They were willing to make sacrifices to hand down to their children America's heritage of freedom and opportunity.

The heroic example of those brave pioneer men and women is full of inspiration for all of us. Let us remember the words of Theodore Roosevelt, when he said: "The old pioneer days are gone. But the need for the pioneer virtues remains."

Replace Relief with Jobs

NO PEOPLE can make headway where great numbers must be supported in idleness. There is no future on the relief rolls. The law of this world is that man shall eat bread by the sweat of his brow. The whole American people want to work at full time and at full pay. They want homes, and a chance for their children, reasonable security, and the right to live according to American standards. They want to share in a steady progress.

There is much discussion as to whether reform of our social and economic system should go before recovery, or whether recovery should precede reform. My answer is that the greatest reform that we could have is recovery.

The nation has not made the durable progress, either in reform or in recovery, that we had the right to expect.

For it must be remembered that the welfare of our people is not recorded on the financial pages of the newspapers. It cannot be measured in stock market prices. The real test is to be found in the ability of the average American to engage in business, to obtain a job, to be a self-supporting and a self-respecting member of his community.

The emphasis on relief has obscured the fact that employment, not aid, is our larger problem. The clinching proof of the New Deal's failure is that almost as many persons are out of work today as there were when it first set up shop in 1933. The key to real stability is not boondoggling, but permanent jobs with the laborer worthy of his hire. Theories will not produce them, nor can unemployment be made to vanish overnight.

All this continuous experimenting and piling up of one uncertainty onto another keeps business upset and holds back undertakings that would bring more jobs. For more jobs is the only real solution to the relief problems, jobs that will allow people to keep their self-respect and plan for their own and their children's future.

"Help Wanted" signs will blossom out of restored confidence in the nation's finances. Work for those who want it comes from the assurance to business and industry that they may plan wisely for the future. Employment comes from the common conviction that the American system of representative government is secure. Confidence is far more important than the exploitation of a multiplicity of pretentious plans which do not work.

The destruction of human values by this depression has been far greater than the American people suffered during the World War. When the depression began,

millions of dependable men and women had employment. They were the solid citizenry of America; they
had lived honestly and had worked hard. They had
dealt fairly with the government which, in turn, had
depended upon their support.

Then they found themselves deprived of employment by economic forces over which they had no control. Little by little they spent their life savings while
vainly seeking new jobs.

We shall undertake to aid these innocent victims of
the depression. We must have a change in attitude and
policies that will give encouragement to the person
who is trying again to become self-supporting.

The WPA program has slammed the door to employment on public works to everyone except permanent relief clients. As a result, those who might other-
wise have become self-sustaining have been forced back
on relief in order to obtain temporary employment.

There are cruel implications in the present program.
Two changes are imperative. One is the decentraliza-
tion of relief. The other calls for encouragement to the
person who is trying again to become self-supporting.
Such efforts must not be penalized as they have been
in the past. In many communities practical ways of
meeting this need have been found. The Federal Relief Administration has ignored these successful local
efforts which restored self-support without injury to
the American standard of living. A shortsighted Federal Relief Administration continues to exhibit utter
unfamiliarity with what has been achieved in these di-
rections.

The remedy for unemployment is not a permanent

dole. Of course, relief must be continued as long as the need for it exists. The American remedy for unemployment is real work at good wages. It is clear that limitation of production and destruction of crops is not going to provide this kind of work.

Our problem of unemployment will not be solved by rabid partisanship, on the one hand, or wishful thinking, on the other. We may differ as to methods and procedure, but there can be no difference as to the imperative necessity for a solution.

Fundamentally, we must always keep in mind that the answer we seek is not based alone on the query, "Am I my brother's keeper?" The solution rests on considering it in a major sense from the viewpoint of a problem created by the rapid development of our industrial machine.

The problem is national in scope and should be solved on a national basis. This involves the most careful consideration of the limitations of the federal and state constitutions.

Solving this problem of unemployment is both humane and economic and we shall solve it in spite of our past neglect and recent well-intended but utterly unworkable, hastily thrown together, makeshift legislation.

Relief without Politics

OUT of this depression has come, not only the problem of recovery but also the equally grave problem of caring for the unemployed until recovery is attained. Their relief at all times is a matter of plain duty.

We of our party have pledged that this obligation will never be neglected. In extending help, however, we will handle the public funds as a public trust. We will recognize that all citizens, irrespective of color, race, creed or party affiliation, have an equal right to this protection. We would consider it base beyond words to make loyalty or service to party a condition upon which the needy unemployed might obtain help. Those who use public funds to build their political machines forfeit all right to political consideration from true Americans.

To me, the most deplorable thing about the present relief setup is the way in which it has been made a matter of wretched party politics. In my opinion, relief should be above politics. It is a matter of fundamental Christianity, and let me say here and now that I, for one, am dedicated to the proposition that henceforth no American citizen shall ever again be put in a position where he has to sell his vote for bread.

After three years of experimentation, relief still remains in chaos. The intentions of the Federal Relief Administration, under the various initials by which it has been identified, may have been high and noble. The political manhandling of the projects, however, has been nothing short of shocking. Idealists may have been at the front door preaching social justice, but party henchmen have been at the back door handing out the jobs.

Taking at their face value the solemn promises of the administration that politics would be kept out of all relief activities, I continued as governor of Kansas the relief organization of my distinguished Democratic predecessor. We thought differences over methods could only injure the deserving. So we accepted what was offered and made an administrative success of federal plans equaled by few other states. The records will show that no state cooperated more fully with the Federal Relief Administration than Kansas.

With the passage of the five-billion-dollar relief bill, however, came the melancholy discovery that a non-political administration of relief was not intended. The WPA was organized so that relief might be handled in familiar "pork barrel" fashion. It has permitted a party machine to spend the greatest peacetime fund in all human history. Our people are disappointed and amazed. They realize now that the promise to make human needs the sole guide for action has been broken. Victory is in the hands of the party spoilsmen.

Nonpolitical relief administrators have been forced out. Citizens have poured the evidences of intolerable conditions upon Washington. The only result has been loss of poise and a resort to abuse by the administration and its spokesmen, who take the undemocratic attitude that all criticism is abuse and that all who do not agree with them have base motives and selfish purposes. They seem to forget that true democracy thrives on honest criticism.

It has been said that the demands for relief have imperiled our federal finances. That is only a half-truth. The money actually reaching the unemployed and impoverished has not rocked the Treasury. The rocking has been done by abysmal waste through changes of policy, maladministration and ruthless partisanship. Relief appropriations have been more than ample, but all too many on relief and work projects have been denied adequate aid because bureaucracy has eaten up too much of the funds intended for relief. We need desperately a cheaper, simpler and more responsible relief administration throughout the union.

Let me emphasize that, while we in the Republican party propose to follow a policy of economy in government expenditures, those who need relief will get it. We will not take our economies out of the allotments to the unemployed. We will take them out of the hides of the political exploiters. The question is not as stated by the administration—how much money the American people are willing to spend for relief. The question is how much waste the American people are willing to stand for in the administration of relief.

The original idealism of the relief program has been wrecked by confusion, contradiction, delay and miserable party politics. The obligation to deal fairly with every person in want seems to have been forgotten. Waste and diversion have melted away the funds intended for those in need—and in need, many times, through no fault of their own. Any government eventually fails unless it deals justly with its most humble citizen.

The centralization of control in Washington has brought about a lamentable and costly breakdown of local responsibility. State governments have been deliberately short-circuited. Local governments have been tempted to sacrifice their rights and their responsibilities, in order to get any share in the distribution of federal funds.

Federal financial aid was obviously necessary in our recent emergency, but every community knows best how to care for its own. The federal relief program has lacked the flexibility to meet local conditions. In many cases, the way it has been carried out has denied aid to truly deserving. In other instances it has encouraged too many to become chronic indigents.

If there is any place more than another where common sense in government is needed, it is in the relief problem. Although many millions of our people still depend on relief and the outpouring of billions is greater than ever, I do not believe that the problems presented are unsurmountable in this land of potential plenty.

Sound Administration and Sound Money

A NATION will survive to correct its political mistakes. But if an unsound financial policy is coupled with them, the nation faces destruction.

We must have a sound and stable monetary system. We must not spend more than we can afford. We must cut down our debts, and stop making new ones. A leaky engine cannot pick up speed. If we are overburdened by debt, we cannot go forward. In a word, we must persevere until we have balanced our budget.

After all, however liberal we are, whatever progressive instinct tempts us and inspires us, common sense and sound policy tell us that we can be only as liberal as we can afford to be and pay our debts and live in decent self-respect.

All this is true in our personal and private affairs. It is no less true in governmental business. Unpleasant though it may be, we must heed the warning from year after year of federal deficits. Waste, extravagance and indecision will not remedy slipshod national housekeeping.

There must be a revival of confidence in national credit, confidence in soundness of the dollar, confidence in the government at Washington. These guarantee the perpetuity of our American system of democracy, and under that guarantee will come a flood tide of recovery.

A financially responsible administration never loses sight of the fact that it acts at all times as a trustee of the people.

It watches every dollar it spends to be sure that it is used in the way it will do the most good. It borrows no more than is absolutely necessary, for it knows that if we exhaust our borrowing capacity today, our children will be helpless should they be called on to face an emergency.

In my judgment these are the common-sense principles that our federal government should follow. Unfortunately they are not the principles which have been followed by the present administration.

Instead, its record is the grim proof of the financial vortex into which we are being drawn.

In spite of the repeated assurances about a balanced budget—in October, 1932; after the banking holiday in 1933; in January, 1934; in January, 1935; and in January, 1936—what has happened?

The administration has continued to increase expenditures, even for the regular departments, and to carry us deeper and deeper into debt. The assurances repeat the old story—"business is improving, revenue increasing, no new taxes will be necessary to balance the budget." How can anyone really believe this in the face of the record of the present administration? The gap between income and outgo steadily widens.

It has piled deficit upon deficit.

It has increased our public debt until today the total is equal to two-thirds of the annual income of every man, woman and child in the United States.

It has created an atmosphere of spendthrift generosity that has made it impossible for it to restore economy in government expenditures.

It has acted as if it were willing to give the whole Treasury away, trying to enrich everybody by impoverishing everybody else.

If persisted in, these recurring deficits inevitably will lead to one of two courses.

One way is inflation. That is a primrose path at the beginning, but there is an inescapable pitfall at the end. Inflation can only culminate in wiping out the savings of the American people.

The first whiff of inflation is pleasant. But inflation grips nations as insidiously as drugs do individuals. The consequences are the same. Most nations that have exposed themselves to the inflation habit have been unable to stop short of utter breakdown. The real victims have been the very ones the inflationary program pretended to help.

The Republican convention advocated "A sound currency to be preserved at all hazards." I agree that "the first requisite to a sound and stable currency is a balanced budget." The second requisite as I view it is a currency expressed in terms of gold and convertible into gold.

I recognize, however, that the second requisite must

not be made effective until and unless it can be done without penalizing our "domestic economy and without injury to our producers of agricultural products and other raw materials."

Comparable to inflation, the other wasteful way out of this financial mess is the imposition of federal taxes more severe than any before known. Even the imposition of these severe levies, if coupled with continued reckless spending, would give only temporary relief. Overtaxation would take its toll in the lowering of our standards of living and the ultimate exhaustion of our resources.

But—courageous leadership can blaze a third path. This road leads to economy and sound administration. It leads to the reemployment of millions of men and women now out of work. If we have the courage to take this road, we must make a far more intelligent use of the federal budgetary system than now is being done. There must be more effective budget-making by the executive. Congress must find a way to consider federal expenditures as a whole, rather than as isolated and apparently unrelated departmental expenditures. Finally, we must consider not only "Where is the money going?" but "Where is it coming from?"

If the money is spent we must get it somehow, some way. If we spend what we do not have today, we must pay the bill tomorrow. Every time we put off present obligations, we mortgage future rewards and future opportunities.

Our government must follow the principle of preparing for the rainy day. In our own families we all recognize the importance of doing this and we try to build up individual reserves.

In the case of the government the equivalent of these reserves is the ability to borrow. It protects this ability by keeping its financial house in the best possible order.

How does it do this? In periods of good times, the government pays off its debts, so that if necessary it will be able to borrow again. It keeps its taxes as low as possible, so that there will be a reserve of taxpaying ability which can be called upon to meet emergencies. It permits its citizens to prosper, so that they will not have to go to the government for aid at the first breath of ill-wind. These are the policies to be followed in good times. In bad times certain changes are necessary.

Every right-thinking person sincerely desires to see the need for relief to the unemployed speedily pass away. Until that time comes, it is reasonable—and nothing less than just—that the government exert all its powers to prevent suffering among the less fortunate. The need only places on us a greater responsibility for sound administration and careful management.

What our nation really needs today is better house-keeping. Our women could show the way. They have had more successful experience than any political spendthrift in getting full abundance out of living and in managing to put by something for a rainy day.

The time has come to put an end to these irresponsible policies. We must establish a system of simple, honest bookkeeping. We must return to the principles which we follow in the handling of our own finances.

This will give us a government able to meet every reasonable demand made upon it; a government fully prepared to assume its increasing financial responsibilities; a government able to meet the needs that arise from any emergency; a government that will leave our children a fair chance to solve the problems that arise in their time.

That is the kind of government we must have if we are to get rid of unemployment by giving our workers real jobs at good pay.

I know that accomplishing all this is not a task that can be completed overnight, and I make no such promise. We have huge responsibilities that we must continue to meet. But with the help of a courageous country it is a task that can and will be done.

That is my pledge to the American people.

Taxing the Poor

IT HAS always been my belief that the government should raise the major portion of its revenue from direct taxes levied on the net incomes of individuals and corporations. When this is done everyone pays his fair share and knows just how much the government is costing him. I have constantly worked for legislation in Kansas to prevent concealment of the cost of government.

On the other hand, if the major portion of the government's income is obtained from indirect and hidden taxes—taxes upon such things as food, clothing, gasoline and cigarettes—then the main burden falls upon those of small income and the cost of government is hidden. In this case, it is the wage earner, the salaried worker, the farmer, and the small businessman who have to pay most of the bill.

Now, let us turn to the record and see just who is paying the cost of our government.

What do the figures of the Treasury Department show? They show that, in the year 1932, 59 cents out of every dollar collected by our federal government was secured from direct taxes. The other 41 cents was collected from indirect and hidden taxes, paid, for the most part, by people with incomes of $25 a week or less.

That was for 1932. Four years later, what do we find? We find that 51 cents out of every dollar collected by the federal government came from hidden taxes.

In other words, the share of the cost of government falling mainly on those with incomes of $25 a week or less has increased 25 per cent during the three years of the present administration. They are paying far more than their rightful share of the cost of government.

Any housewife can tell you this, because the housewife knows, better than anybody else, how the mounting cost of living is curtailing the comforts of the home. And you cannot long fool her with the pretense that only the rich will pay.

And just how have those with small incomes paid more? When we consider the government as a whole—federal, state and local—we find that they have paid in a thousand different ways. Already the average family spends one-fourth of its income for taxes, whether the family knows it or not.

Take bread, for example. When we buy a loaf of bread for ten cents we pay about eight cents for the bread. The other two cents goes for taxes.

If we smoke a package of cigarettes a day, we pay $22 a year in taxes.

So it is in all our spending. We cannot buy a stitch of clothing without the government's taking in taxes

a part of the money we pay out. We cannot buy an
ounce of food at our grocery store without being taxed
to support the government. We cannot go to a movie,
or to a baseball game, or ride in a motorcar without
this invisible tax arm of government reaching out and
taking a part of the money we spend. This has been a
growing tendency of government in recent years.

Most of these taxes, it is true, are hidden so deeply
that we cannot see them. But the taxes are there just
as truly as they are in the sales tax on gasoline. They
cost just as much, and are just as real, as they would
be if they were taken right out of our pay envelopes.
These hidden taxes—federal, state and local—amount
to about 20 cents out of every dollar we spend. In the
case of the federal government alone, they amount to
over $5 a month for every family.

It is in this way that the government's financial policies affect us as individuals. The more the government
wastes, the more money it has to take from us. The
more it takes from us the less food and clothing we
can buy for ourselves, the less we have for the education of our children and the less we have left to set
aside for meeting emergencies—for the building of
homes, for improvement of farms, for the construction
of factories.

In short, every dollar that the government takes
from us in taxes means just one dollar less for us—a
dollar that we might use to buy things, the production
of which would create jobs.

This hidden tax increase has come despite the fact
that the tax rates on incomes of individuals and corporations have been raised. It has come despite the fact

that they are paying far more actual money into the Treasury than they did in 1932. In other words, the larger payments by well-to-do individuals and corporations have not been enough to cover the waste and extravagance of this administration. What is the result? Those of our citizens with small incomes have had to pay an increased proportion of the cost of the federal government.

Unfortunately, now as always, there are people today calling themselves liberals who regard any suggestion of economy as reactionary. They seem to think willingness to throw other persons' money around without any consideration of value received is a peculiar sign of a pure heart. They show too little consideration for the toil which millions of American men and women will have to undergo in order to pay off the debt so gaily incurred.

━━

C   H   A   P   T   E   R   N   I   N   E

A Legacy of Debt

THE present administration has entirely disregarded a fundamental principle—that you can't go on indefinitely spending more than you receive. It is paying half of its bills with borrowed money. The truth is we are living in a fool's paradise—far beyond our income.

We all know this cannot continue indefinitely, because we have known persons who have tried it. We have seen them go along for a while with apparent ease, buying first one thing and then another which they could not afford. And then we have seen them wind up "on the rocks."

Whenever a government continues to live beyond its income, it will suffer the same fate. For a while there will seem to be no end to the money which the government can spend. But in due time the day of reckoning must come.

We must remember that every time the government ⌐pends a dollar, that dollar will have to be paid by us or we must pass the debt on to be paid by our children.

No parents like to leave their children a heritage of debts and mortgages. But the creation of a staggering public debt closes the door of opportunity to the youth of America, just as certainly as a staggering private debt.

We must face the issue squarely. The present administration's daily mounting deficits are closing the door of opportunity to your children and to my children.

How is it that the government has been able to follow such a will-o'-the-wisp financial policy? It is because the public has not been properly informed.

We have been told that all this extravagance will be paid for by "soaking the rich." This is not possible. The figures of our Treasury Department show that if we confiscated all incomes in excess of $5,000 a year, it would not be enough to pay for the cost of our federal government.

Do not think that we have been getting something for nothing as the result of the huge government spending of the past three years. Some of the debt, it is true, has been shifted to the wealthy, but the major portion of the debt, both the principal and the interest, is being charged up against ourselves and our children.

A simple inquiry into the facts and figures will show that our growing debts and taxes are so enormous that, even if we tax to the utmost limits those who are best able to pay, the average taxpayer will still have to bear the major part. While spending billions of dollars of borrowed money may create a temporary appearance of prosperity, we and our children, as taxpayers, have yet to pay the bill. For every single dollar spent we will pay back two dollars!

There is no other group to whom we can shift the burden, and it is a burden that gets heavier and heavier every day that the present wasteful policies of the administration are continued.

Crushing debts and taxes are usually incurred, as they are being incurred today, under the guise of helping people—the same people who must finally pay them. They invariably retard prosperity and they sometimes lead to situations in which the rights of the people are destroyed. This is the lesson of history, and we have seen it occur in the modern world.

There are some people who seem to believe that the government can create money. That is not true. All it can create are promises to pay money. This is what it does when it issues paper money or sells bonds. In principle, this is similar to what we do when we open a charge account at a store. We get something now and promise to pay for it later. If we charge more things than we can pay for, our promises to pay become worthless. The same is true of government.

So, if we are to be realistic in our thinking about government finance, we must think of the government as almost a member of our family—a member to whom day by day, week by week, year by year, we must give part of what we receive in our pay envelope or part of the crops we raise.

We must not lose sight of the fact that a public debt is just as much a liability to each and every individual as a private debt. The fundamental principles of government finance are exactly the same common-sense principles that we follow in the handling of our own family finances. So long as our government follows these principles our people will prosper. They will be able to weather depression, drought and other disasters. But if our government disregards these principles, it squanders our resources and destroys the public credit.

That is the legacy the present reckless administration is leaving our children.

Proved in Kansas

IT CAME to us with a sense of surprise that the happenings in Kansas in the last few years had awakened so much outside interest—that the state's record is considered something of a phenomenon because its local subdivisions, city, county, school and township, have managed to live within their means, cut taxes and reduce bonded debt.

If the situation in Kansas seems unusual it is only because the type of government which the citizen has a right to expect has become the unusual in a day of theory and experimentation. What we have done in Kansas is what a sensible family does in the face of reduced income. We have cut out the frills. We have maintained essential services, but at minimum cost. We have insisted that every dollar buy more, not less, of government.

We have learned in Kansas that reduction of taxes does not necessarily mean reduction in public services. We have found that a sound public budget, carefully made and rigidly adhered to, plus a well-considered tax policy, makes it possible to maintain essential government services and still keep expenditures within the bounds of citizens' ability to pay. In 1934, our low revenue year, we spent 42 per cent of the tax dollar for educational purposes, exactly the same per cent of the tax dollar we spent in 1929, our peak revenue year.

We have been through an exceptionally hard and trying period in Kansas. There are many improvements I would like to see made as soon as we can loosen our belt a little. As I said in my first inaugural address, the state which first puts its house in order will be the first on the road to recovery. We have had the same difficulties the rest of the country has had, plus some very special troubles of our own. Preceding the general economic depression, we had a long agricultural depression. We suffered four years of drought, the worst recorded since Weather Bureau records have been kept.

Now, specifically, what has Kansas accomplished toward sound financing in troubled times? In answering the question I must speak specifically as a Kansan and as governor of the state.

Since the peak of 1929, general property taxes in Kansas have been reduced over 32 per cent.

The cost of government was cut 22 per cent for the biennium of 1933–1934 below that of the biennium of 1931–1932.

Counties and communities liquidated 22 million dollars' worth of bonded indebtedness from 1932 to 1934, during which time new bonds, about half of which were for relief purposes, were issued in the amount of 5 million dollars, leaving a net reduction of 17 million dollars in the bonded debt of Kansas counties and municipalities.

The per capita cost of state and local government in Kansas in 1929 was $71—in 1935 it was approximately $52, a reduction of about $19 per capita—or more than 26 per cent.

This was not done by executive proclamation, nor by the legislative branch of the government placing itself in subjection to the will of the executive. The credit does not belong to any one state administration nor to any one political party. It rightfully belongs to thousands of township trustees, county commissioners, school board members, and city officials all over the state who were responsive to the need of their taxpayers.

In 1932, the year preceding my first year as governor of Kansas, all state and local revenues totaled 127 million dollars. By 1934 they had shrunk 30 million dollars, or about 24 per cent, and were reduced to about 97 million dollars. This was a period when our state did assume heavy relief burdens.

Our constitution provides that the county government must make levies and raise funds to take care of such persons as have been on relief in the last three years. Kansas has the record of complying promptly with every request of the national relief administrator and in cooperating fully in every way. We did not believe in putting relief into politics.

Throughout 1933 and 1934, according to the report of the national relief administrator, 30.6 per cent of the relief burden was financed from nonfederal funds furnished chiefly by the county and local governments.

This 30.6 per cent of nonfederal funds in Kansas compares with twenty-seven states which contributed less than 25 per cent of their own relief moneys and fourteen states whose contributions to their relief funds were less than 10 per cent of their total relief expenditures. Kansas ranked fifteenth among the states in per cent of nonfederal funds used for relief in this two-year period. Despite this added burden, the tax load in Kansas was reduced.

This lifting of the tax burden was made possible by the loyal cooperation of state and local officials. It is generally conceded, however, that new state legislation adopted was a vital part of the general program of economy. The legislature proceeded with the welfare of the state in mind and both political parties cooperated in enacting this legislation.

Three pieces of legislation are of special interest:

First: "The Cash Basis Law," which prevents our spending what we do not have.

Second: "The Tax Limitation Act," which limits the total amount of levy.

Third: the new "Budget Law" which makes the building of governmental budgets a really democratic procedure, known to all, instead of a star chamber proceeding known only to insiders and understood by only a few.

The cash basis law is explained by its title. Under the old "no fund warrant system," when a treasury became empty, officials simply issued warrants marked with the words, "no funds." These warrants bore interest and were taken by banks. Presumably they were to be liquidated eventually out of tax funds. In fact, that system had encouraged local political units, which spend many millions of dollars annually, deliberately to unbalance their budgets, year after year, without providing any time of reckoning.

When the cash basis law went into effect it revealed an indebtedness the magnitude of which never had been previously realized by the taxpayers. It is now necessary for school boards, township officials, county commissioners and all political units therein, to limit their spending to the actual income of the current year. The cash basis law has attracted much attention.

A member of the Harvard University faculty declared that Kansas had blazed a new trail in legislation aimed to put local government on a business basis. When we talk of balancing public budgets, we usually think of the federal budget or the state budget. However, the seed of sound fiscal policy must be planted in the smallest political subdivision—or it is likely not to be found at all.

As part of the general program our tax limitation law was codified and strengthened so as to put a new and reduced limitation upon the sum total levy which can be fixed by any particular political unit. Of course this limit can be adjusted by future legislatures as conditions may require.

The new budget law strengthened and clarified an act already upon the statue books. Under this act, the taxing unit must prepare a budget of proposed expenditures, post a copy in the community for the taxpayers to see, publish it in the local papers, and hold a hearing upon it. This law tends to take budget-building out of the back room, and place it under the scrutiny of the taxpayer.

Without the cash basis law, however, the budget law would go only a small part of the way. To compel local subdivisions to build a public budget and submit it for inspection, hearing and approval—is fine. But if the subdivision is not compelled to stay within the approved budget, then only one of the two major evils has been cured. The cash basis law provides that after a budget has been submitted and a tax levy made, the subdivision cannot spend against anticipated collections, except in cases of emergency for which expenditures must be allowed by the State Tax Commission. The teeth in the law are further sharpened by the provisions that any public officer who violates it is automatically removed from office.

I want to stress on this point that this was not accomplished by the head of the state government; it was not done by a central government. It was accomplished by more than 8,000 taxing boards, from the state legislature down to one-room school district boards, making separate levies for school purposes in the peak revenue year of 1929. Five years later, in the depth of a depression, and caught between droughts and dust storms, the same 8,000 taxing boards, each operating separately, set aside for school purposes the same percentage.

No order was issued, no state law directing such a division was enacted, no person, board or commission set the figure. Eight thousand and more school boards and other taxing agencies, each dealing with its own situation, attained the same combined percentage in prosperity as in adversity.

To my mind that accomplishment is more than an interesting coincidence. In it is expressed a large part of my faith in local self-government and in the capacity of the people to govern. The combined decision of the common people frequently approaches closer to applied wisdom than the intellectual superiority of so-called leaders.

To understand what has been accomplished in Kansas one must appreciate the innate ability of Kansas people to govern themselves. At times, under the stress of state problems, I go and stand before a great mural in one of the rooms of the governor's office. There is pictured a sweeping conception of the spirit of Kansas. A prairie schooner, drawn by yoked oxen, rumbles its slow way across the plain, while beside it, unafraid and uncomplaining, trudge fathers and mothers and children. Underneath are those stirring words by Whittier:

> *We cross the prairie as of old*
> *The pilgrims crossed the sea,*
> *To make the West, as they the East,*
> *The homestead of the free!*

"The homestead of the free!" How easy it is for that homestead to become the homestead of the bound and not the free—if bad government and unsound fiscal policies saddle the homesteader with a tax load he cannot carry.

The errors of other administrative policies may not

of themselves be fatal, but the errors of an unwise financial policy have always been fatal to every government in the history of civilization.

We all admit that our modern industrial state is complicated, and far from the simple structure of our founding fathers. But does the fact that we have changed and grown make it wise to abandon, out of hand, the course which the wisdom of our forefathers charted for us, not out of theories, but out of the stern and bitter realities of economics and statesmanship?

If the wind rips the roof off a house out in our country, we don't tear down the walls, also, and abandon the whole structure. We put on a new and better roof —strengthening those parts which we have discovered to be weak. Similarly, we must not abandon what remains of our American institutions or jeopardize the remainder of our freedom simply because an economic storm has devastated our nation and shaken confidence. Rather let us replace what is destroyed, rebuild what is torn away, and in so doing strengthen our structure in every way that experience can suggest. That is common sense—horse sense, as we say in Kansas. Let us be certain that we are making only those changes which are real improvements—changes dictated not only by wishful theory, but by the stern teachings of experience. Let us put experience, that greatest teacher of all, back on our governmental faculty.

The Farmer and Recovery

NO SOUND national policy looking to the national welfare will neglect the farmer. This is not because the farmer needs or wishes to be coddled, or that he asks for undue help. It is necessary because the needs of a great nation require that its food producers shall always stand upon a social and economic plane in keeping with the national importance of their service.

The present administration's efforts to produce this result have not been successful. Payments under the Triple-A did help to tide farmers over a difficult period. But, even before it was ruled out by the Supreme Court, the Triple-A was rapidly disorganizing American agriculture. Some of its worst effects continue. By its policies the administration has taken the American farmer out of foreign markets and put the foreign farmer into the American market. The loss of markets, both at home and abroad, far outweighs the value of all the benefits paid to farmers.

Worse than this, from the standpoint of the public, is the fact that the administration, through its program of scarcity, has gambled with the needed food and feed supplies of the country. It overlooked the fact that Mother Nature cannot be regimented.

The time has now come when we must replace this futile program with one that is economically and socially right.

Our farmers are entitled to all of the home market they can supply without injustice to the consumer. We propose a policy that protects them in this right.

I am advised from reliable sources that the costs of about 200 items the farmer has to buy are increased about one-fourth by the operation of the tariff. Because the farmer has been forced to sell on the world market, is he not entitled to some countervailing provisions, to some compensating tariff equivalent, in order that he may receive an equal benefit?

The purpose of the tariff is to protect workers and industry from the cheap competition of foreign labor. The farmer should be given this same protection.

Is it any wonder that the immediate concern of agriculture is tariff equality with the other groups comprising this nation? There are supplemental factors which would be helpful to the farmer, such as the greater industrial use of farm products, the rebuilding of foreign markets, and last but not least, lower taxes and interest charges. Even more basic would be an expanding home market growing out of restored confidence in our future.

There is no single solution of the farm problem.

Some of our farmers, dependent in part upon foreign markets, suffer from disadvantages arising from world disorder. Until these disadvantages are eliminated, we

propose to pay cash benefits in order to cushion our
farm families against the disastrous effects of price
fluctuations and to protect their standard of living.

Low prices have been caused by the practical loss of
the farm markets, both domestic and foreign. Of the
markets, the domestic market always has been far more
important for our farmers.

But even in the case of the major cash crops, on
which a surplus has been produced, our domestic farm
prices have largely been fixed by the prices bid by our
foreign purchasers. In other words, the surplus has set
the price for the whole crop.

The problem of agriculture certainly must be ap-
proached on a nonpartisan basis. No one can justify
any attempt to make political capital out of the national anxiety for effective solution of the agricultural
problem.

The Republican party's farm program as a whole
will be made to serve a vital national purpose.

The family type of farm has long constituted one of
the cherished foundations of our social strength. It
represents human values that we must not lose. Widespread ownership of moderate-sized tracts of land was
the aim of the Republican Homestead Act. This conception of agriculture is one phase of the general principle that we stand for—preserving freedom of opportunity in all walks of life.

The benefits which will be paid under our program
will go no higher than the production level of the
family type of farm.

Now, as always, the basis of our national life is in
the soil. Unless those who till the soil prosper, pros-

perity for their fellow Americans in other walks of life will be short-lived. A mistaken notion seems all too prevalent that American farmers are seeking special privilege. Some people talk as if the welfare of agriculture were separate and independent from that of the nation. Developments of the last decade clearly demonstrate the fallacy of that belief. The farm is woven into our economic fabric. It must be treated fairly if our cloth is to remain whole.

Among all the problems that are pressing for consideration today, if there is one that is truly national it is the distress of agriculture. It has suffered all too much from partisan politics. It is not only a national problem, but a many-sided one. It concerns the family dining table, the factory employment gate, the corner grocery, and the savings window in your own bank. When we more clearly realize how directly it enters the daily life of every family, agriculture will again come into its own.

Over and above the remedial legislation still required, there is much that can be done by informed and sympathetic administration. The discrimination in national policies, against which our farmers so justly complain, must end!

Once we have restored the purchasing power of the American farmer, we shall have gone a long way towards providing work for the unemployed. New jobs would be made available in factories, railroads, and merchandising establishments. On most of the nation's 6 million farms there is need at this very moment for additional labor. There are farm buildings to be painted and repaired. There is farm machinery to be overhauled. There are fences to be built. There are terraces and dams to be constructed.

The farmer has lacked money to do these jobs. He couldn't afford to hire the additional hands. There are many chores that would be shifted from the farmer and his wife to other shoulders, if the family income would permit. Given the buying power he fairly earns, it is not too much to say that the farmer could provide jobs for many of the millions still unemployed and eager to work.

By restoring agriculture to its rightful place in our national life, we shall, also, keep open the door of opportunity on the farm. Thousands of our boys and girls who prefer the farm to the city would make the farm their home and farming their lifework. There they should be able to find the financial independence and the security to which their labor entitles them. The whole country would benefit by restoring this freedom of choice to youth. All would gain by opening this way to a better distribution of population.

The wealth of our soil must be preserved. We shall establish effective soil conservation and erosion policies in connection with a national land use and flood prevention program—and keep it all out of politics.

The proper application of soil conservation principles would help materially to prevent the production of such price-depressing surpluses. As I have repeatedly said, it should be possible to develop a national program of soil conservation on the more than 65 per cent of the nation's crop land which already has begun to lose its food-producing value.

Equally impressed with the public interest is the

problem of flood control. Flood control fits right in with the soil program. According to government studies, a sound national conservation program in itself would reduce the damage from floods 25 per cent.

The situation today emphasizes the urgent need for a sound national land use policy. Our soil must not be exhausted by wasteful methods.

The American people, now as always, are responsive to distress caused by disasters, such as the present drought. The Republican platform reflects that spirit. We shall fulfill its pledge to give every reasonable assistance to producers in areas suffering from such temporary afflictions, so that they may again get on a self-supporting basis.

Practical Progressivism—Opening a Few Issues

IN THE field of government today the word "equality" best describes our main objective.

Freedom of enterprise does not mean that the government shall do nothing. Government must always be on the alert to repress violence and fraud, to terminate special privilege and unfair practices, to protect the everyday American in carrying on projects that are beyond the scope of private enterprise.

We must strive for equality of justice under law; equality for the wage earner and the wage payer in their negotiations; equality in the market place for agriculture. We must insist upon equality of opportunity in every walk of life. This means that government must use all the forces at its command to protect this equality of opportunity from the insidious evils of monopoly.

In this way we can best meet the challenge of the democratic principles underlying our system of government. In this way we can best foster our common interests without forfeiting that fair freedom of individual opportunity which is one of the ideals of American liberty.

Neither under the pretense of promoting efficiency nor to establish class rule are the American people willing to abandon democratic institutions in favor of arbitrary government in any form.

A progressive and practical meeting of the issues will advance us further toward our idealistic objectives than haphazard experiments and vague chatter about social justice. A few immediate issues suggest themselves.

SOCIAL SECURITY—AN OBLIGATION

It is our duty to amend the Social Security Act to make it workable. We recognize that society, acting through government, must afford as large a measure of protection as it can against involuntary unemployment and dependency in old age. We pledge that the federal government will do its proper share in that task.

History and experience alike teach us that "government is protection." When it ceases to protect, it ceases to be government. As a nation, we have begun to protect childhood but the obligation to protect old age lies straight before us. This obligation is the legacy from the machine age in which we live. It is an essential part of the unemployment problem of a great industrial civilization.

Every big industrial nation has had to give that kind of protection. In America we could once handle the problem pretty well, by depending on individual thrift, family aid, local taxation and private contributions. These still have their places, and vital places they are. Some of the more progressive business enterprises have established systems of their own, thus having done some useful pioneer work. But I believe we have reached a stage where government must take a hand. Now, there is one really good point about the administration's effort in this direction—it did stimulate thought and arouse study along these lines. But the complicated legislation it rushed through in characteristic fashion will, I fear, prove to be unworkable in many respects. We shall have to revamp it, and we must take care not to allow the eager desire to make a showing lead us into the temptation of turning out something that will be only another delusion.

THE RIGHTS OF LABOR

Another matter of deep concern is the welfare of American labor. The general well-being of our country requires that labor shall have the position and rewards of prosperity to which it is entitled. I firmly believe that labor has the right to protect this position and to achieve those rewards by organizing in labor unions. Surely the history of labor in the United States has demonstrated that working conditions, wages and hours have been improved through self-organization.

The right of labor to organize means to me the right of employees to join any type of union they prefer, whether it covers their plant, their craft, or their industry. It means that, in the absence of a union con-

tract, an employee has an equal right to join a union
or to refuse to join a union.

Under all circumstances, so states the Republican
platform, employees are to be free from interference
from any source, which means, as I read it, entire
freedom from coercion or intimidation by the em-
ployer, any fellow employee, or any other person.

The government must maintain itself in the position
of an umpire: first, to protect the public interest; and
second, to act as a mediator between conflicting groups.
One of the greatest problems of this country is to
develop effective methods of conciliation.

Taking a dispute, after it gets into a tangle, and
rushing it to the doorstep of the President is a bad way
to handle a labor situation or any other situation.

Under the title of labor, the Republican platform
commits the party as follows: "Support the adoption
of state laws and interstate compacts to abolish sweat-
shops and child labor, and to protect women and children with respect to maximum hours, minimum wages
and working conditions. We believe that this can be
done within the Constitution as it now stands."

I hope the opinion of the convention was correct in
believing that the aims we have in mind may be attained within the Constitution as it now stands. But,
if that opinion should prove to be erroneous, I shall
favor a constitutional amendment to read: "Permit-
ting states to adopt such legislation as may be necessary adequately to protect women and children in the
matter of maximum hours, minimum wages and working conditions." This obligation we cannot escape.

MAKING AMERICA OVER

We hear a lot of talk about making America over. Who is to do it? The government at Washington? I hardly think so. But, the thing that has made America over every generation is the individual effort, the ambition, the courage and character of our people, and the feeling that individual opportunity was open to everyone.

These still are the fundamentals. There are no workable substitutes for them.

I do not mean that we should not be open-minded to change. We're a practical people. We have learned to do a great many things to advantage by pooling our mutual interests.

But cooperative enterprise is entirely different from a planned economy mapped out by a lot of bureaucrats ruling from Washington. This kind of planned society is a sort that has developed under European dictatorships. I don't believe we want anything of that kind over here. This type of centralized planning is based on the idea that the American citizen is not able to take care of himself, and that he requires some man who must tell him what to do and what not to do. I still believe that the American people, under proper government protection, still like to plan for themselves.

GOOD WILL IN FOREIGN AFFAIRS

In international affairs, the Republican party has always worked for the advancement of justice and peace. Following the early tradition of our country, it has consistently urged the adjustment of international disputes in accordance with law, equity and justice. We have again declared our continual loyalty to this principle.

Republican presidents sent delegates to The Hague conferences and one of them took the leading part in the termination of the Russo-Japanese War. Another Republican president called a conference which, for the first time, produced a reduction and limitation of arms on a wide scale. Still another led in securing the treaty outlawing wars.

In purpose and achievement, our party has a record which points the way to further helpful service in creating international understanding, in removing the causes of war, and in reducing and limiting arms.

We shall take every opportunity to promote among the nations a peace based upon justice and human rights. We shall join in no plan that would take from us that independence of judgment which has made the United States a power for good in the world. We shall join in no plan that might involve us in a war in the beginning of which we had no part, or that would build a false peace on the foundation of armed camps.

We need common counsel, common action, in the field of foreign affairs. The method is provided for it, but too often we've neglected to use it. Under our Constitution, as you know, great powers in respect to foreign relations are lodged in the chief executive, but he doesn't stand alone. The final control over the making of treaties is a responsibility of the Senate of the United States, not of a majority, but of two-thirds of the senators present. In this important regard, the minority is given a voice. I believe in that. And, in my judgment, those presidents have been well advised who have made it their practice to consult not only the Department of State and the majority members of the Committee on Foreign Relations, but the minority members as well.

FREEDOM OF THE PRESS

Much has been said recently about freedom of the press. There is, however, another danger which should be guarded against, and that is the suppression of information affecting the public welfare.

I don't like secrecy in governmental affairs.

Suppression of news at its source is as dangerous to American institutions as government control of news at point of publication.

AN EXAMPLE OF INDIVIDUALISM—THE MEDICAL PROFESSION

From the earliest days, the general practitioner in America was, first of all, an individualist. The circumstances of his work made him that; but it was a fortunate situation for the people who needed medical care. It meant that they could have personal ministration, that there was an intimate relationship between physician and patient and that the sufferer became at once, and remained, the object of very special attention.

Down to the present day American medicine has continued to be primarily individualistic. It is chiefly on that basis that it is to be distinguished from medicine in many foreign countries. I know very well the arguments for an extension of the best of medical service to all groups of the American people. It is a worthy cause. It is enlisting the attention of the best brains of the profession.

A nation that can maintain and even elevate its medical standards and the state of public health in the trying years of a prolonged depression needs to make no apology for the quality and the reach of its medical facilities.

That condition itself is a tribute to the American physician in his continued unselfish devotion to a worthy task.

Medicine will not willingly be made the servile instrument of politicians or the instrument of domineering bureaucracy. I predict that the typical American physician and organized medicine as a whole will at no time be ready for any scheme of impersonalized medicine which is totally alien to the best traditions of the American practitioner and of the profession as a whole.

CHAPTER THIRTEEN

The Spoilsmen Must Go

THE Republican party has pledged itself to the merit system and to its restoration, improvement and extension. In carrying out this pledge I believe that there should be included within the merit system every position in the administrative service below the rank of assistant secretaries of major departments and agencies, and that this inclusion should cover the entire Post Office Department.

We must build a new and better civil service that will fill government positions with trained, trustworthy and capable employees, and offer to our youth a career in public service based on merit and qualifications for the job. The political spoils system, and the spoilsmen responsible for it, must go, in the interest of economy and efficiency.

There never was a time when government so needed factual information and expert trained service. We must not allow our rising prejudice against mere experimentation to blind us to this fact. In Kansas we have found that a research department to collect facts

—not to administer theories—is of the greatest importance and aid to members of the legislature and to the chief executive of the commonwealth as well.

Thousands of workers are necessary to administer the affairs of a nation of 130 million people. Grover Cleveland, and every other president since the Civil Service Law was enacted, extended its scope by executive order. So, too, each Congress has opened up new avenues for the activities of the Civil Service Commission. This steady advance of the merit system for half a century was halted and turned back three years ago by the political spoilsmen now in power.

These spoilsmen have seen to it that not one in a hundred, out of the 235,000 new jobholders added by this administration, has been bothered by merit requirements. But worse than that, the morale of the whole federal service has suffered as the result of ousting thousands of trained employees from their hard-won civil service status. Their faith in the protection of the merit system has been ruthlessly betrayed. The time has come to end this political debauch.

The merit system must be restored, expanded and improved, and the extension of the system must include the opening up of higher positions within the federal service to advancement through merit.

Building a better and broader civil service will raise the standards of both administrative and legislative branches of the federal government. It will not only give us better administration, but it will give us better legislation. It will enable our legislators to concentrate on legislation, and not be compelled to waste so much time on the distribution of patronage.

Millions of honest citizens will support a party that is not trying to perpetuate itself in power at the expense of the taxpayers.

CHAPTER FOURTEEN

The Challenge of Monopoly

THERE should be regulation of industry wherever regulation keeps opportunity open and protects, not hampers, the people as a whole in the exercise of their rights. I refer to such things, for example, as the protection of childhood and of women in industry, workingmen's compensation, enforcement of sanitary conditions, proper lighting and ventilation, compulsory safety devices on machinery, and reasonable working hours. The definition may be expanded to cover all sorts of antisocial practices.

The remedy for monopoly and special privilege is to do away with them. This must be one of our first objectives.

One of the chief causes of our economic difficulties is the tendency of monopoly to fix prices and retain special privilege. Great markets yet to be developed lie within our own borders and across the sea. The frontier of new wants points the way to a better standard of living in this country. Even in our own most prosperous days many of our people did not live well enough.

How can it be said that we have overproduction when so many Americans are badly fed, badly clothed, badly housed? How can it be said that we have overproduction when large groups of our fellow citizens are neglected, underpaid, or unemployed? How dare we talk about overproduction when the evil effects of these conditions run beyond the tragedy of stunted lives and challenge the welfare and the honor of the nation?

My experience has convinced me that monopoly is bad for everyone, including business itself. Men in a monopolistic position aren't on their toes, fighting. Prices are fixed and maintained so high that buying power is shut off. If technical improvements are made, the profits aren't generally fairly passed on to labor and to the consumer. All the other groups outside the fold of monopoly, particularly agriculture, are put at a disadvantage, and opportunity is closed to the small man. We have to attack the evils of monopoly frankly and resolutely and require the government to keep a fair competitive system in force at all times. It will not do to think that we can put monopoly on its good behavior, and forget about it.

For most of my business life I was an independent oil producer. I brought new wealth out of the ground in the form of a raw product. Then my problem was to market it. So, as a small independent oil producer, I was always coming up against concentrated wealth in the shape of big oil companies, pipe-line companies, and railroads. Naturally, I became conscious of the problems of monopoly, of the power and tendencies of big aggregations of capital. I suppose it's human for a businessman to want to get into a position where he can fix prices and eliminate competition, perhaps by friendly agreements or the influence of size. He imagines it will make things easier for him. But he only defeats his own purpose and creates a generally intolerable condition.

Freedom of the Classroom and Free Speech

AS A parent and as the chief executive of a state I have had to deal with education, and have learned something about the problems and dangers that face free education today. I have learned that it is best to meet them squarely and with complete frankness.

Let me give you two of my fundamental conclusions at once, conclusions that I have reached as a citizen and as governor of Kansas.

In Kansas we believe that our schools—public, parochial and private—must be kept free of all control by the federal government.

In Kansas we insist that no teacher should be required to take an oath not required of all other citizens.

The right of free inquiry is one of the essentials of free government. It is the very bedrock of democracy. In Kansas we believe in academic freedom and we practice it.

We must ever remember that academic freedom, political freedom, religious freedom and freedom of opportunity are all bound together. Infringement upon one will soon lead to infringement upon the others. In fighting to maintain our freedom we will make our greatest progress by fighting for the freedom of all.

We should not overlook the fact, however, that today, both at home and abroad, men are striving for power through leadership of the mob. Because of this, I believe that our educators should make a more than normal effort to see that our youth is given a background of our heritage and tradition—a fundamental understanding of the form and philosophy of our government. If this is done, we need have no fear of allowing our youth to study any and all systems of government to which their curiosity leads them.

Only through ignorance or bigotry can we be destroyed. With understanding and intelligence, our future citizens will be able to separate truth from the ever-increasing amount of propaganda.

We Americans are still in control of our destiny. We can remain so only through the processes of sound education.

We must not be afraid to follow the truth, wherever it may lead. Our attitude, in its broad application, must remain that expressed by Thomas Jefferson. In explaining the aims of the University of Virginia, he said: "This institution will be based on the illimitable freedom of the human mind. For here we are not afraid to follow truth wherever it may lead, nor to tolerate error so long as reason is left free to combat it."

I believe that a teacher has a right to the same freedom of speech in expressing his political, social or religious convictions as any other citizen.

And I believe that a teacher has the same right to work for the accomplishment of his political and social ideals as any other citizen.

This does not mean that a teacher should use a class-room to put forward his own pet views and theories, at the expense of other views and theories. If he does, he is no longer a teacher; he is a propagandist. Our schools must always be institutions where views are expressed free of the personal prejudices of the teachers. Upon this I am, I believe, in complete agreement with the opinions expressed in resolutions by the teachers themselves through their own associations.

Our system of free education has failed if class distinctions are allowed to develop in this country. We must look to our teachers to see that they do not develop.

Today, perhaps to a greater degree than ever before, the control of our educational institutions must be kept in the hands of the local communities and the educators themselves. For we may as well face the fact that the tide is running against free government today. In many lands, the hand of the government is closing down upon education. It is being made into a tool, for autocratic purposes. In these countries free inquiry in the pursuit of enlightenment for its own sake is being destroyed.

In these days of widespread propaganda, it is imperative that our teachers be kept free and that our educational institutions, our newspapers, and the radio be kept independent, either from control of autocratic government or from the influence of any selfish interest.

There must not be censorship of what is spoken or

written, and, equally important, there must be no control of the source of news.

But let me say here, it is to our everlasting credit that most of the great gifts to our educational institutions have been made without any strings attached. They have been kept singularly free from political influence or bureaucratic control.

An excellent example of the freedom which exists today in our educational institutions is the active interest always taken by educators in our social, political and economic problems. In some instances, the arguments and conclusions advanced by our institutions of learning have jarred the viewpoints of those who are unable to see the necessity for change.

But many examples could be cited of progressive policies in government and in business, which have had their origin in our educational institutions. This is as it should be.

If education is to realize its true goal, it cannot confine itself to an academic discussion of life—it must become part of life itself. I believe education is making a great contribution to the solution of our difficulties.

Next to our government, our educational system is our greatest public effort. It has been well termed our outstanding success. The development has taken time, it is true. The processes of a democracy are always slower than those of an all-powerful government. But they are likely to be more certain of good results.

As you all know, it took the efforts of a full generation to win the fight for free public schools supported by tax levies. In this fight the humiliating pauper school laws were the first to go. Then, after more years of effort, we wiped out the last law, which by levying charges upon the parents denied schooling to the children of the poor. This meant that we at last recognized that an education is the birthright of every American child, that to provide for it is a common obligation of the community and of the state. This principle is the foundation upon which our tax-supported public school system has been built.

At the same time, our schools have kept pace with the developments of modern life. The school of today faces the problems of more complex conditions. Under the direction of a better educated and no less devoted teaching corps the public schools have gone far beyond the three R's. They have developed this way with the full approval and support of their public—a public which has always stood ready to undergo sacrifices to give adequate training to the future citizens of America. My own state, for example, devotes more than 40 per cent of each tax dollar to the support of the schools, and other communities and states act with corresponding liberality.

One rung after another has been added to the ladder of free public education. It is a truly democratic ladder. Given the ability within himself, the child from any home can aspire to climb to the highest rung.

This freedom of educational opportunity has been one of the priceless assets of American life. It has been one of the great unifying forces of our nation. It has helped to train the people for our kind of government. It has maintained democracy at the grass roots.

No one can study this record without being impressed by the imagination and constructive genius of the American people. In every sense, this movement for free public schools came from the people themselves.

At each stage responsibility remained close to them. At no point has the federal government been required to assume charge. Because our people felt that the school system was their own, their interest in education has always been maintained. They wanted schools that would give their children better opportunities than they themselves had enjoyed, and they were willing to make sacrifices that they would not make for any other public purpose.

Objectives

IN THE Republican party we do not believe that the people wish to abandon the American form of government.

We propose to maintain the constitutional balance of power between the states and the federal government.

We propose to use the full power of the federal government to break up private monopolies and to eliminate private monopolistic practices.

In other words, the Republican party proposes to restore and to maintain a free competitive system—a system under which, and only under which, can there be independence, equality of opportunity, and work for all.

A free competitive system is necessary to a free government. Neither political nor civil liberty long survives the loss of economic liberty. Each and all of these liberties, with the precious human rights which they involve, must be preserved intact and inviolate.

The Republican party must again look forward,

confident that there is in the American people the will and intelligence to master our problems.

Our party has before it the opportunity to be the servant of the nation in that effort. As I understand the spirit of our party today, it distinguishes between progress and mere change. I believe that in the business of government, good intentions are not enough. Our high national ideals, the call for social justice, our goal of maximum individual opportunity for every man, woman and child in the land are all being betrayed by wasteful, slipshod, incompetent, happy-go-lucky administration. The people are being given half a loaf, and charged for a full loaf.

Progressive government deserves something better than casual experiments. It can succeed only when accompanied by careful preparation, competent administration and sound fiscal policies.

The Republican party must go forward along sound and progressive lines, prepared to find honest solutions for the problems that confront us. No other course will do. No other ought to be considered. We should make it our object to restore a fair and decent opportunity for every man and woman who aspires to such an opportunity. Where humanitarian legislation is needed, we must provide it. Where labor or agriculture is under disadvantages, these must be removed. Where business is being hamstrung, so that it cannot furnish goods or jobs, we must free it. We must insist upon equal rights for all, special advantages for no interest or group. That is simple justice. That is also the only way we can prevent the rise of class feeling, which I am sorry to see is being fostered in high places.

I pledge myself, so far as it lies within my power, to protect our American heritage of freedom and opportunity. We want every boy and girl to have a better chance in life than we had. We want a government in Washington that will safeguard for the younger generation the opportunity to develop, each in his own way, the American qualities of self-reliance, of honesty, and of generosity. We must remain a nation of free citizens, each choosing for himself, each holding fast not only to opportunity, but to the truths he has inherited. This—an America of free and independent citizens, recognizing our mutual obligations, one to the other—is the America we should strive to leave for our children.

The citizen who assumes the direction of the executive branch of our government takes an oath that he will "faithfully execute the office of President of the United States, and will," to the best of his ability, "preserve, protect, and defend the Constitution of the United States." This oath carries the obligation so to use executive power that it will fulfill the purposes for which it was delegated.

No man, in common good faith to his fellow citizens, may rightfully assume the duties of the high office of chief executive and take the oath that goes with the office, unless he shall intend to keep and shall keep his oath inviolate.

If I am elected chief executive of this nation I propose to restore our government to an efficient as well as constitutional basis.

I shall call to my aid those men best qualified to conduct the public business—and I mean just that.

I shall stand back of them.

I shall hold them responsible for doing their jobs.

I shall cooperate wholeheartedly with Congress in an effective reorganization of the numerous government agencies, to get rid of those that are not necessary, to eliminate duplication, to insure better administration, and to save the taxpayers' money.

I hold that it is the right of our people to have their greatest public-service enterprise—their government —well administered.

These are some of the aims and proposals of a Republican administration that would enter office under a pledge to conduct the public business with honesty, frugality, courage and common sense.

In common with all my countrymen, I look forward to the America that is to be

It should be a nation in which the old wrong things are going out and the new right things are coming in.

It should be a country which produces more and more until there is plenty for all, with a fair chance for all to earn their share.

It should be a land in which equal opportunity shall prevail and special privilege shall have no place.

It should be an America that will bring to bear the whole of her great spiritual force in a common effort to drive the curse of war from the earth; an America that, for the sake of all mankind as well as ourselves, will never lose the faith that human freedom is a practical ideal.

It is in these aims and in these works that I vision the manifest destiny of America. Everything we need for their realization we can find, I firmly believe, within the principles under which this nation has grown to greatness. God grant us, one and all, the strength and the wisdom to do our part in bringing these things to pass.